Franc

ois Nepveu

The hidden life

François Nepveu

The hidden life

ISBN/EAN: 9783741142406

Manufactured in Europe, USA, Canada, Australia, Japa

Cover: Foto ©Andreas Hilbeck / pixelio.de

Manufactured and distributed by brebook publishing software (www.brebook.com)

Franc

ois Nepveu

The hidden life

The Hidden Life,

BEING EXTRACTS TRANSLATED

FROM

NEPVEU'S

PENSÉES CHRÉTIEN~~NES~~

London:
J. MASTERS, ALDERSGATE ST.
1869.

Dedicated
to
Two Sisters
who, by a loving Submission,
and Perseverance in Well-doing,
have exhibited both Aspects
of a
Life of Devotion.

Translator's Preface.

THE following extracts are translated from a popular French work, which has received high praise from one whose judgment carries great weight—Dr. Newman.

Its chief recommendation lies in its being thoroughly practical and containing much matter in a small compass.

The quotations from the Fathers have been rendered from the Latin, and not the French.

May some readers of these pages, dissatisfied with that cold, unloving propriety which characterises the easy religion of the day, and yearning after higher things, be led to a more zealous imitation of CHRIST and the Saints of old. May they realize in an increasing degree—taught perhaps of sorrow and bitter disappointment—that after all there are better gifts and higher rooms of service than the heaping up of riches, the winning of titles, and self-seeking of every kind.

They need not wander far in search of work. All are not called to uncommon labours. All need not exchange their homes and their home duties for cholera wards and the fever-stricken dens of our great cities; but *whatsoever thy hand findeth to do, do it with thy might; do it heartily as unto the Lord.* We need not despise little things, for they have made great saints. The Gospel tells us of Mary the Penitent washing her SAVIOUR's feet and wiping them with the hairs of her head, but of Mary the Blessed—the holiest doubtless among women—not one striking action is recorded, so that her life may almost be summed up in these words, *she found favour with God; and, a sword pierced through her soul!*

Even they whose field of labour lies within the narrowest limits—nailed perchance to a sick bed—can give a good example, love, and prayer. And what is more powerful for good than these? "The best way to correct the faults of others is to correct our own;" example is more winning than many words; while love and prayer combined can move heaven and earth.

Changes—social, political, and religious—are in store for England. Our future depends more, under GOD, upon the zealous co-operation of Clergy and Laity in every good work than upon the wisdom of legislatures and the valour of armies. True religion is the backbone of a people. Let us then all do our part—some with ten talents, others with but one; let us live for GOD, and love GOD, and He *shall be our shield and exceeding great reward,* and shall show us in His own good time and way "that lowly self-knowledge is more to be prized than the highest attainments of science, and that to mortify and conquer our own appetites in however trifling instances is more praiseworthy than to storm strong cities, to defeat mighty armies, work miracles, or raise the dead."[1]

M. J. B.

Trinity Sunday, 1869.

[1] "The Spiritual Combat,"—S. Francis de Sales' favourite pocket companion, of which there is an excellent and cheap English translation.

Contents.

	PAGE
Sincere Repentance	1
Backsliding	3
Humility	4
Faith and Practice	5
Grace abused	7
The Judgment Day	8
Of giving Offence	9
Impurity	10
Occasions of Sin	12
Lukewarmness	13
Little Sins	15
Sufferings	16
Prayer	17
Neighbourly Love	18
Conformity to God's Will	19
Zeal	20
Salvation our great Business	21
Fidelity to Grace	22

Contents.

	PAGE
Besetting Sins	24
Pleasures	25
Slander	26
Paradise	27
Relapses	28
Blindness of Heart	30
Self-Surrender	31
Faithfulness in Trifles	32
Lively Faith	34
Trust in God	35
On loving Christ	37
God's Will	38
God's Glory	39
Penitence	40
Covetousness	41
Lukewarmness	42
Christ's Love	43
Born again	45
Heaven	46
Bad Example	47
Occasions of Sin	48
Frequent Communions	50
Prayer	51
Following Christ	53
Christ's hidden Life	54
Neighbourly Love	55
Conformity to God's Will	57
God's Presence	58
The Measure of Grace	59

Contents.

	PAGE
Salvation a hard Task	61
Duty	62
Hardness of Heart	63
Marks of Lukewarmness	65
Reverence in Church	66
Sufferings	67
The Love of God defined	68
Humility	69
Mortification	71
Besetting Sins	72
Backsliding	73
Temptation	74
Almsgiving	75
The Magdalene	77
Mortification of the Flesh	78
Trust in God	80
Lukewarmness	81
Union with Jesus in the Eucharist	82
Meekness	83
Penitence	85
Repentance delayed	86
Holy Communion	88
Humility	90
The Elect	91
Impurity	92
Crucified to the World	94
Sloth	95
Meditation	97
Repentance	98

Contents.

	PAGE
Idleness	101
Temptation	102
The single Eye	104
The one Thing needful	106
Our Only Mediator	108
Recollectedness	110
Habitual Sin	112
Excuses of Non-Communicants	114
Sufferings improved	115

THE HIDDEN LIFE.

Sincere Repentance.

TO be sorry for past sins is not enough. There must be a firm and sincere resolution never to commit them again. A half-hearted 'willing,' and feeble 'purposing' are not enough. Hell is paved with them. They can make men unhappy, but not penitents. To rest content with a vague liking for good and dislike of evil, is to trifle and deceive oneself. A true penitent does not say, "I would," but, "I will, and I shall do it, cost me what it may." Good intentions are fruitless when they imply merely a conditional willingness to do right. When a man says, "I would," he means, "I would consent to give up this or that sin, were it not necessary at the same time to give up this or that pleasure or object." " I would" means here—GOD is urging me by His inspirations to forsake the sin, and I mistake the promptings of Divine grace for those of my own heart; bare sentiment for deliberate consent; ineffectual desires of conversion, for actual conversion. Resolutions must be carried into effect. Many persons think they 'will' a thing when they conceive feeble desires respecting it. He however who is really determined to give up a sin, takes measures accordingly, however painful and difficult; overcomes all obstacles, however arduous; avoids all occasions of temptation, however much they may fall in with his interests or tastes. Reader, hast thou renounced sin after this fashion? Then thy resolution was sincere, and thy penitence genuine.

Fatal error, to mistake the work of grace for our own work.—*S. Bern.*

Backsliding.

FREQUENT relapses cast a doubt on the genuineness of a man's repentance. He may rely on the sincerity of the confessions of his sins, and say that if he falls, he, at least, raises himself again through penitence. But the genuineness of that penitence is questionable which allows a man to fall again as soon as he has risen. Though the will be liable to change, it does not pass at once from one extreme to the other; from a sovereign loathing of sin, such as must ever be found in true penitence, to as strong a love of it, as is the case in deadly sin when the creature is preferred to the Creator. *They* are not implacable foes who are so soon and so easily reconciled. *That* is not a radical cure which admits of so speedy a relapse. No, frequent relapses look suspicious. The invariable result of genuine repentance is a fresh supply of grace which imparts great strength to resist the allurements of sin, and prudence to avoid those occasions which may lead to temptation. When then a fatal facility for committing sin, and a careless disregard of all precautions are found, we may reasonably assume that grace has not been received, and that the repentance has not been genuine.

It is folly to wish and not perform.—*S. Bern.*

Humility.

WE should be grateful to GOD for having made salvation depend not on self-exaltation, but on self-abasement. Every one cannot exalt, but every one can abase himself. All cannot do great things, or form vast designs for GOD's glory; but there is not one who cannot humble himself. All have not the gift of prayer in an eminent degree; but who cannot humble himself in prayer, and thus achieve much while he seems to labour in vain? I cannot always do all the good I would, but I can always acquiesce in my inability, and humble myself before GOD on this account, and so supply that which was wanting in my actions.

I cannot (literally) *pray without ceasing*,

but I can incessantly humble myself. O humility! short but sure way of working great things in a brief space.

More justified in GOD's sight was he that condemned himself, than he that proclaimed his own righteousness.—*S. Aug.*

Faith and Practice.

MAN'S faith is GOD's glory. We honour GOD's law by submitting our wills to those dispensations which run counter to our inclinations; by loving that which the natural man loves not, as for instance, the person of an enemy. We honour the Divine wisdom by yielding ourselves to His guidance, even when He leads us by a way we have not known, and in a direction opposed to our tastes and interests. We honour the Divine truth by believing that which cannot be tested by the senses, nor conceived by the reason; which is even opposed to the experience of the one, and the light of the other.

Our faith honours GOD when our practice harmonises with it. To believe in a Being infinitely great, and yet not to serve Him; infinitely good, and not love Him; infinitely righteous, and not fear Him; infinitely holy, and sin against Him,—is this consistent? To believe that what is highly esteemed among men is abomination in God's sight, and yet to hanker after all this; believe that Christ has denounced woes against the rich and voluptuous, and eagerly desire to be such; believe that He blessed poverty and the tears of repentance, and fly from them in dread; believe that Heaven is reached through humility, and wish always to be exalted; that a Christian must crucify the flesh, and think only of pampering it; that the Kingdom of Heaven is taken by force, and spare oneself the least hardship,—is this to act consistently?

Let us either change our faith or our practice. To believe these truths and not practise them is infidelity. *He that believeth not*, saith the Saviour, *is already condemned*, but he that believes, and yet lives as though he believed not, shall be still more rigorously punished. Barren faith shall only increase our condemnation.

It is imposture when faith and practice disagree.—*S. Amb.*

Grace Abused.

NOTHING is more needful than grace, and yet there is nothing which we abuse more. Nothing is more precious, and yet nothing is more despised. The smallest measure of grace is worth more than all the blessings and pleasures of the world. The price paid for grace was the precious Blood of our Redeemer. As often then as we abuse grace, we trample under foot the Blood of CHRIST; and His death, far from being the instrument of our salvation, becomes the aggravating cause of our reprobation! When we become insensible to the secret reproaches of conscience, when we stifle salutary remorse, close our eyes to the clear light of grace, and neglect the urgent inspirations of GOD's Spirit, do we reflect that we are resisting, despising, and outraging grace? Think we of the dangers and the consequences of such a sinful course? Or shall we begin to think of them when the evil is past remedy? The damned in hell set its full value upon grace, and eternally bewail their abuse of it. Had we received no grace, we had not been guilty, and had we received less grace, we had been less guilty. But, as it is, the poor heathen shall be thy judge, weak and lukewarm Christian, for if he had received but a small portion of those graces which GOD has lavished upon thee, perchance he might have become a saint. And since they have not made of thee even a Christian, they shall make thee a reprobate.

Not grace alone, nor man alone, but grace working with man will save.—*S. Aug.*

The Judgment Day.

IN that day CHRIST alone shall appear great in holiness. In His presence all the works and virtues of the world shall disappear; and as at dawn shadows and darkness disappear, so at the sight of JESUS CHRIST all heathen virtues of which pride and false notions of honour have been the motive; all good works of which caprice, or passion, or interest, or the praise of men, or vanity, have been the principle, shall disappear. JESUS CHRIST, saith S. Paul, is the one *foundation*. No virtue or holiness which is not built on Him can *abide*. Those palaces so magnificent in appearance, but which are not founded upon Him, shall fall in that day; the fire which must destroy the universe shall consume them like straw in a moment. Gold alone, or, in other words, that which rests on CHRIST, shall *abide*.

Alas! how many actions which now appear so illustrious and brilliant in the eyes of men, shall appear unrighteous when tested by the one infallible standard—the righteousness of CHRIST.

So powerful on His Cross, what shall He be on His Throne?—*S. Aug.*

Of Giving Offence.

YOU have stolen a piece of gold. There is no hope of salvation for you unless you restore it. You have taken away your neighbour's innocence and purity. How will you make compensation for this cruel wrong? You have robbed JESUS CHRIST of souls so dear to Him that He shed for them His precious Blood. Can you expect any mercy at His hands unless you make compensation for all this? The transports of joy felt by the SAVIOUR on finding His lost sheep enable us to judge of His grief at the loss of one. How is it then that we take so little pains to satisfy and appease an offended GOD? Hast thou then no fear of hearing the same words that Cain heard, "*The blood of* this poor *Abel*, of this innocent one, *thy brother* and mine, whom thou hast corrupted and destroyed, by robbing him of purity and grace, *crieth unto Me for vengeance against thee?*"

An accurate account shall be rendered of thy bad example.—*S. Aug.*

Impurity.

IMPURITY is looked upon as mere frailty, and a venial sin; and yet there are few sins more grievous in themselves, none more fatal in their results. It is that leaven, which appearing nothing in itself, *leaveneth the whole lump*. (Gal. v.) It works like the almost unfelt sting of a snake, which instils its deadly venom into the whole frame, and gives the heart its death-blow. Unless we fly from this snake how can we escape being bitten? Unless we fear it, do we not deserve to perish? It is a property of impurity to multiply itself in a marvellous way. It may also be considered the source of almost all the sins and crimes which desolate the world. There is no sin which GOD has more severely punished. It provoked the most awful vengeance ever inflicted by GOD on man. The waters of the flood were sent to quench the flames of lust. The fires of Heaven fell on the infamous cities of the plain to remove the least trace of their abominable impurities.

Mournful perversity, that sells to the Devil for a moment's pleasure a soul bought with CHRIST's Blood. *S. Aug.*

Occasions of Sin.

THE heart is like a citadel which the demon cannot storm except by a surprise or by tampering with the garrison. He gains over our affections by presenting to view some interest, by the attraction of some pleasure, or by the promised reward of some coveted distinction. Now these things have not much power over us when absent; when however circumstances present them before us, they powerfully influence our senses and affections; and these in turn entice the reason and captivate the will. Men are for the most part moulded by the influences which surround them. They are good or bad according to circumstances.

Avoid then every occasion of sin if thou wouldst avoid sinning. This is the easiest and surest way. GOD has condescended to our frailty in making our salvation and victory depend on anxious precautions, rather than on courageous resistance. Fear then, and thou shalt be safe; fly, and thou shalt gain the victory.

A gracious Providence has made victory depend on fear and flight.—*S. Cypr.*

Lukewarmness.

LUKEWARMNESS is a very dangerous state. There are persons towards whom God cherishes a special affection, and whose path is watched by a special providence. Blessed with virtuous tendencies, a happy disposition, a noble spirit, a sound heart, an upright understanding, they are prevented with abundant grace, and stung with remorse for the least fault. Such persons cannot be mere average Christians. They must belong to God altogether, or not at all. They must be saints, or they will be reprobates.

Lukewarmness is a state of blindness in such persons, which springs from the frequent commission of apparently trifling faults, from want of recollectedness, and from the indulgence of the besetting sin. Thus a false standard of right and wrong is set up, and great sins are accounted trifling faults.

Then lukewarmness is dangerous because it is in a manner incurable. It is easier to convert a great sinner, than a lukewarm professor. A soul thus blinded ignores both the disease and its consequences; and therefore betakes itself not to the proper remedy. Its case resembles that of persons in delicate health, in whom some vital organ is secretly affected. Such persons, because they do not suffer much, and live like their neighbours, are blind to their danger, neglect the proper remedies, and are brought to their graves before they have realised that they are ill. Similarly the lukewarm, because they can show some good works, and commit no gross (though perhaps grievous) sins, either seek no remedy for a disease of which they see not the consequences, or the ill-success of the means hitherto tried makes them loath to try them again, or the remedies themselves lose their power and are of little use.

I have seen the cold and carnal become hot and spiritual, but the lukewarm barely ever.—*Cassian.*

Little Sins.

NOBODY becomes wicked all at once, but by accustoming oneself to commit some little sin, which always bears some relation to deadly sin, one gradually familiarizes oneself with it. It is viewed with less horror, then it is less feared, then it is witnessed in others without much indignation or surprise, then it comes to appear somewhat pleasant, and at last the sin is committed readily and with a feeling of delight.

The commission of little sins does not indicate irremediable backsliding, but a going astray; not an absolute rupture, but a growing cold which predisposes to a rupture. By accustoming oneself to neglect GOD, one comes by degrees to despise Him. Genuine love does not become hatred all at once, but weak love soon becomes indifference, indifference in turn becomes coldness, and coldness hatred. Distraction in prayer seems but a small matter, and yet often results in deadly sin.

Trifling faults grow into deadly sins.—*S. Bern.*

Sufferings.

THOSE who love and serve God only in prosperity are mere Jews; but those who love and serve Him in the furnace of affliction are true Christians. Has Jesus Christ not proved His love for us in enabling us to acquire virtues by furnishing us with opportunities for their practice? For how can virtue be acquired without practice? And how are patience, gentleness, self-denial, humility, charity, and conformity to God's will to be better practised than in time of suffering? Sufferings are at once the most efficacious means of acquiring virtues and the surest evidences of their genuineness.

Again, did not Christ prove His love by enabling us to acquire a conformity with Himself crucified in order that we may hereafter be like Him in glory; by helping us to add fresh lustre to our heavenly crown, and to gain each moment fresh degrees of glory?

In what way then can we show our ingratitude more than in making His greatest favours a subject of murmuring and discontent.

Our very chastisements are favours, what then shall the favours be when He hath ceased to chasten.—*S. Aug.*

Prayer.

PRAYER can never fail, since it rests on the goodness of GOD, and the faithfulness and merits of JESUS CHRIST. It is as impossible for prayer duly offered not to be effectual, as it is for GOD'S goodness, or CHRIST'S merits to fail. CHRIST has not only promised, but He has sworn that we shall obtain all that we ask in His name. Was it needful that He should swear with an oath in order that we might believe? What an honour GOD does us when He swears on our behalf? How dishonourable it must be to Him when we will not trust His very oath! Why then do we pray with so little faith? The eternal FATHER owes us everything because the SON has given up everything for us. He cannot give us too much since there is nothing which the merits of His SON cannot claim for us. If then we remain poor, with so rich a treasury to draw upon, must not the fault be ours?

Prayer is omnipotent; singlehanded it can do anything!—*Theod.*

Neighbourly Love.

IN the law GOD had commanded men to love their neighbours, and JESUS reiterated this command, and, at the Last Supper (when He was as it were making His will) He repeated it three times, as if to mark how much He had it at heart. By the observance of this commandment, and not by the working of miracles, not by the gift of tongues, not by faith itself, were His true disciples ever after to be known. Bearest thou this character stamped upon thee? Thou mayst have faith enough to move mountains, courage enough to undergo martyrdom, and yet *without this* thou art not CHRIST's disciple. Thou hast not His spirit because thou hast not charity.

Lovest thou Him whose precept thou contemnest?—*S. Aug.*

Conformity to God's Will.

SIN is the only evil which GOD wills not, but yet He wills its results. He condemned the envy of Joseph's brethren, but yet He willed its result, namely, Joseph's servitude. The fury of the Jews filled Him with horror, but yet He willed and ordained the death of His SON. And in like manner He will punish the wrong which thou art suffering, but yet He wills the loss and affliction which it causeth thee. We may indeed regret such evils when viewed merely by themselves, but how shall we murmur against the will of GOD? It is GOD's will. Important words! What further reasons does a man need who believes and loves GOD? Dare a Christian say, "GOD wills this, and I will it not?"

The will of GOD, being infinitely wise, does everything at all times in the best way, and chooses the best means of arriving at the end proposed, although sometimes the means He uses appear most likely to defeat the ends. Thus, for example, He destroyed the sin of the world through the greatest of all crimes—Deicide.

Let us then adore His inscrutable designs, and believe that He orders all things for the best, and can do more than we can comprehend.

An evil hath happened to thee; well, thank GOD, and lo! it is a blessing.—*S. Chrysost.*

Zeal.

THE world shall henceforth teach me how to serve GOD. The conduct of worldlings shall be my example and rule. I will learn of them how zealously I ought to serve GOD. What will they not do, what not suffer, to please the world? How disgraceful it is that we should do less for GOD than the world's followers for it! Less for our salvation than they for their perdition! The thought of hell ought surely to quicken our zeal. Shall we count any task too laborious which can save us from eternal fire? We sear with a hot iron a wound which endangers life; what ought we not to endure, then, when eternity is at stake? Again, the thought of heaven ought to stimulate us. No sacrifice should appear too costly which is to gain for us eternal bliss. Can anything stir us up more to do all the good we can, than the thought that the most indifferent action, when done for God, earns for us the possession of God; and that our recompense in heaven shall be exactly proportional to the zeal with which we have employed every moment of our lives in some useful work. If a merchant had a limited time allowed him during which he might realize enormous profits, would he lose a single moment?

Be as zealous for the world's Maker, as thou hast been for the world.—*S. Aug.*

Salvation our Great Business.

PROPERLY speaking our salvation is our only concern, because it is nearly the only thing which we alone can accomplish, which at least cannot be wrought without our help. God created us without our co-operation; but even He cannot save us without it. Everything can be done by proxy, except the work of personal salvation. And yet in other matters we do not trust so much to our friends as to ourselves. We naturally think we shall manage them best, being the most interested parties. And, however much we may seek the support of Providence in our temporal concerns, we think ourselves bound to second it with our own efforts. In the matter of salvation alone do we leave all to GOD, as if He could do everything and we nothing. And yet He can effect everything without our co-operation except this one thing—our salvation. We cannot indeed be saved without His grace, but His grace cannot save us without our co-operation.

Thou didst not help to make thyself, but thou must help GOD to save thyself.—*S. Aug.*

Fidelity to Grace.

GRACE is the voice of GOD speaking to us. With what a loving and teachable spirit should we not listen! It is a visit which He pays us; with what respect and humility should we not receive Him! It is a seeking; what sentiments of corresponding gratitude should we not feel! And yet we do the very reverse of all this each time that we are faithless to grace. How then shall GOD punish this slight? If we will not hear, He will keep silence—a silence more to be dreaded than the loudest menaces. Receive Him not, and He will withdraw,—a withdrawal more fatal than the angriest strokes. Repel Him, and He will desert us,—a desertion more cruel than the fiercest penalties.

Grace is the price of the Blood of CHRIST, the fruit of His death. If it be the price of His Blood, how should we prize it! If the fruit of His passion and death, how should we hoard it! To resist grace is to tread under foot the Blood of CHRIST. Shall that Blood thus trodden under foot not cry, louder than the blood of Abel (not for mercy as it would have done had we valued it, but) for vengeance?

It is our part to yield to grace, it is GOD's to reward us for yielding.—*S. Aug.*

Besetting Sins.

FEW are without some besetting sin. The most virtuous are not those who have none, but who combat it best. It *must* be known, it must be conquered. If it be not, it will conquer us. There can be no truce with this enemy. Victory alone can purchase peace, and, with it, our salvation; for this sin is the source of almost all our other sins. We must cut off the head of this Goliath if we would vanquish the rest of the Philistines. Their total defeat depends on that of this redoubted enemy. The besetting sin prevents our knowing the other sins, which it makes us commit, or at least their enormity. All sin blinds, but especially the besetting sin. All that we eagerly desire appears right to us; consequently penitence is made impossible. No remedy is sought for an unfelt evil. Moreover this sin is the principle of almost all our actions. It enters into all our thoughts and aims. Strengthened by being so often brought into play it becomes a habit; and then a necessity. As a matter of fact, how few persons do we see give up a besetting sin or an inveterate habit! Art thou not still the slave of that sin which held thee twenty years ago? Nay, hath it not tightened its grasp?

A perverse will becomes a ruling passion, and this in time becomes a necessity.—*S. Aug.*

Pleasures.

PLEASURES are remedies. They must not then be hurtful, dangerous, or continuous. Not hurtful, for what fearful blindness it is to make one's supreme happiness consist in that of which we must hereafter repent bitterly, or eternally perish? Not dangerous, for what sensible man would take a dangerous remedy when sick? What must we think then of persons who indulge readily in many pleasures, which, though not wrong in themselves, are, as experience tells, very dangerous? Pleasures, again, must not be continuous, for remedies cease to be remedies when taken for a long period. A ceaseless round of pleasures enervates the mind, and weakens the spirit; and, by inducing a state of indolence, causes the simplest duties to be viewed with repugnance and dislike.

Pleasures flatter the eye, but poison; their enjoyment is sin, and their reward death.—*Eucher.*

Slander.

SLANDER, though a common sin, is none the less grievous. It inflicts three mortal wounds at one stroke. It wounds the speaker by depriving him of charity, which is the life of the soul. It wounds the person assailed by blighting his good name and by filling him with unchristian resentment. It wounds, lastly, the bystander, by instilling the poison into his ears, and by rendering him a partner in guilt through his readiness to hear. Like assassination, it is the act of a coward, who attacks secretly those whom he dare not assail face to face.

Slander, like an arrow, flies lightly and wounds readily, but is not readily withdrawn.—*S. Bern.*

Paradise.

WHAT is Paradise? It is a blessing not merely beyond our labours and merits, but our thoughts and desires; which *they* only can conceive, who possess. It is the most marvellous invention of GOD's wisdom, the term of His liberality, the price of His blood; a blessing so great that GOD's Almightiness can give us nothing better; for with it Himself He gives, and what better thing *can* He give? It is a region whose inhabitants have none other portion than GOD Himself, but who, in possessing GOD, possess all things. In Paradise we shall see GOD face to face because there shall be no veil between us and Him; possess Him securely, because we shall never fear to lose Him; love Him ceaselessly, perfectly, wholly, because He shall fill our hearts. We shall rejoice in Him without satiety, because in Him we shall ever find fresh beauties, ever taste fresh pleasures. Seeing and possessing GOD we shall grow like Him, holy, pure, wise, mighty; transformed into Him, we shall have the same wills, affections, and desires; all in all to us, we shall find all in Him.

"He alone, O LORD, who understandeth Thy Nature and Thine Excellency, can understand what Thou hast prepared for them that love Thee. When, O JESUS, shall I enjoy that blessedness of which Thou art the Source and the Object? When shall I behold Thee face to face, not as in a glass darkly? When wilt Thou fill my soul with that torrent of delight which refreshes Thy holy city?"

We shall enjoy but One; but that One shall be everything to us.—*S. Aug.*

Relapses.

WHENCE comes it that we are perpetually falling back into the same sins? Is it not because we are not resolutely determined to break with our sins? Do we believe a sick man when he says he wishes to be cured, and yet will take no remedies? Possibly we are ready to take some remedies, but not the most suitable ones, because they are too violent and irksome. Does this not show that we are not in earnest in our determination to abandon sin? If we were asked to employ these remedies for some violent bodily disorder, would we hesitate a moment? Would they not appear easy? Whence comes it then that they appear impracticable where our conversion is concerned, if it be not because in the one case we are in earnest, and in the other we are not?

But, (say some) the obstacles are stronger than the remedies, and this is the cause of relapses.

But what are these obstacles? Have we ever tried to overcome them? Have we made a serious effort to conquer that passion which draws and entices us to sin? Are we not carried away after making the slightest possible resistance? These obstacles are no doubt great; but if your goods, your health, your lawsuit were at stake, they would not bewilder you as they do now when it is a question of avoiding sin. Whence the difference? In the one case we are in earnest, in the other not. And yet if we are not sincere in our resolution to avoid sin, neither is our repentance sincere.

Penitence is vain when sin dogs its steps.
—*S. Aug.*

Blindness of Heart.

BLINDNESS of spirit and heart is the ordinary *cause* of sin. Could a man, if he knew the horrible nature of sin, how opposed it is to GOD, how fatal to himself, prefer it to GOD? Could he, if he considered what infinite calamities follow as its necessary consequences, make it his sovereign good? *Lord, that I may receive my sight.* (S. Luke xviii.) "Open mine eyes, enlighten my spirit, cure my blindness. May I see Thy mercies, to love them; my own abject misery, to scorn myself; and all the hideous deformity of sin, to hate and to avoid it!"

But blindness is the *effect* as well as the cause of sin. It begets it and is in its turn begotten by it. When sin enters a man's heart it blinds him. Hence it is that we see so many men, enlightened and prudent in other respects, so blind as regards all saving truths. Wise in everything else, they are fools in the matter of their salvation; and yet what shall all the rest profit a man, if he lose his soul? Blindness is a *penalty* of sin.

The sinner, saith the SAVIOUR, will not come unto the light; GOD to punish him, abandons him, and grants him his heart's desire. The sinner delights in darkness; GOD inflicts upon him judicial blindness.

GOD sheds penal blindness over forbidden lusts.—*S. Aug.*

Self-Surrender.

HAPPY the soul which abandons itself to the conduct of GOD! It feels sure that GOD will never leave nor forsake it, though every creature may. When GOD guides and protects what can harm?

The perfection of self-surrender to the conduct of GOD is shown in its practice where it appears most contrary to our interests and inclinations. Our principal, or rather our one desire must be to follow the will of GOD. Nay this must be done, even where we see not the reason. The will of GOD is reason enough; any additional reason rather weakens the merit by weakening the absoluteness of the surrender. All

Lively Faith.

FAITH without works only justifies GOD in condemning us. *He that believeth not is condemned already;* but he that believes and acts not in accordance with his faith shall be still more condemned. The barren fig tree is cut down and cast into the fire; the unprofitable steward who has buried his talent is cast into outer darkness. CHRIST gives no other reason for the condemnation of nominal Christians in the day of judgment than the *omission* of works of mercy. *I was an hungred, and ye gave Me no meat,* shall be said to those who *shall go away into everlasting punishment.* (S. Matth. xxv. 42, 45.)

Do good then. Not to do it is to do evil. A useless life is a sinful life. Act up to the measure of your light. According to your light shall be the rigour of your judgment. Do as much good as you have done evil, and you will do much. Do all the good you can. Limit the good you do, and you limit your love to GOD, and His goodness to you. Do good zealously, for *Cursed is the man that doeth the Lord's work deceitfully.* Do it with a pure intention, else good becomes evil, *light* changes into *darkness.* (S. Luke xi. 35.) Do it with the help of grace, else it will have no merit. And when you have done all, say, *We are unprofitable servants; we have done that which was our duty to do.* (S. Luke xvii. 10.) How many persons have *leaves* without *fruit,* the appearance of virtue without the reality; mistake the results of a happy temperament, careful education, worldly sense of honour, desire of men's praise, or a purely heathen morality, for the fruits of holiness; and live useless lives, neither giving themselves up to the practice of Christian virtues, nor the exercise of works of mercy.

The life is not idle when the heart is busy.—*S. Ambr.*

Trust in God.

WE cannot distrust self, or trust God too much. It is not surprising that God grants everything to lively faith; for nothing proves our love more. Do we not trust those we love and those who love us? Nothing proves better our estimate of His goodness, power, wisdom, and foresight. The power of GOD is never so conspicuous as when it gathers light out of darkness, and brings the greatest marvels out of nothing; and faith shines brightest when the very motives for despair are made so many reasons for hoping, and when, like Abraham, a man hopes against hope. A man thus upheld, never fears less than when he has everything to fear; never hopes more than when his circumstances are desperate; never abandons himself more unreservedly to GOD's care, than when all the world, and apparently GOD Himself have abandoned him. It is then that he can say with Job, *Though He slay me, yet will I trust in Him;* yes, I will lean on the arm that smites me. However great the evils which threaten, nothing is more to be feared than faithless fear.

A Christian believes in the impossible.— *Tert.*

On loving Christ.

CHRIST longs for our love! It is as marvellous in a GOD to desire our love, as in us to refuse it.

He leaves nothing undone to obtain His desire. He invites by promises, enlists by appeals to self-interest, wins by favours, solicits by prayers, yea, compels by commands, and constrains by threats. His longing for our love is a plain proof of His exceeding great love for us; while the faintness of our desire to love Him is as plain a proof that we love Him not. Did we love Him, we should feel how worthy He is of love, and we should thus long to love Him more; feel pained at our lack of love, and eagerly embrace every means of augmenting it. The hardest ways would become easy in our eyes, and we should exclaim at every moment, "Thy love, my JESUS, Thy love and nothing else. Alas! how far removed am I from feeling this perfect love! Thou only, my SAVIOUR, canst at once give me this ardent desire of loving Thee, and render it effectual."

Thou LORD commandest me to love Thee, grant what Thou commandest, and command what Thou wilt.—*S. Aug.*

God's Will.

OUR perfection consists not in praying, fasting, toiling, or winning souls, but in doing GOD's will. Those acts however excellent in themselves, if they be not ordained of GOD are disorderly; if not animated by this motive, are imperfect. The best become faulty, when done *apart from* the will of GOD, and the most indifferent become excellent when done *according to* it. *There is a time for all things.* It is not always seasonable to practise penitence, or mortification, to pray, or labour; but it is to do GOD's will. And we do it when we keep His commandments, follow the motions of grace, do our duty in our state of life, and *obey them that are over* us. But it is not enough to do GOD's will, we must do it *as*, and *when* He wills. To do it otherwise, is not to do it at all. So then to pray when we are required to act, to talk when one should keep silence, is not to do GOD's will.

This rule of constantly having GOD's will in view is the shortest and surest way of becoming holy.

How shall our perversity and His uprightness agree?—*S. Bern.*

God's Glory.

NOTHING is more glorious than to glorify GOD. To serve so exalted a Master is to reign. What is the glory of the greatest conquerors compared with the glory of GOD? The prayer of faith, humiliation patiently undergone, mortification duly practised, every good work of what kind soever, provided it be done to the glory of GOD, is greater and more glorious than the most important transactions, and the government and conquest of an empire. Do we believe this? Why then do we omit so readily pious exercises, or discharge them so remissly?

He shall ever cleave to the dust who

reckons anything great except the One, Eternal, Infinite Good.—*Imit. Christi.*

Penitence.

IF penitence hath its harsh, it has also its pleasant aspect; if ever accompanied by pain, it is often followed by greater consolations; its tears are not always bitter, and a sinner sometimes finds more satisfaction in weeping over his sins than he found in committing them. If it is a sad thought to a penitent that he has irritated God and exposed himself to all the consequences of His wrath, it is a sweet one that the Saviour compassionates his tears, and grants him that pardon which is never refused to a *broken and contrite heart*. If it is sad to be agitated by the motions of unruly passions, frightened at the sight of sins committed, and stung with remorse, it is sweet to see sins blotted out, remorse assuaged, and troubles succeeded by a great calm.

Nor is this all; the Lord fills a penitent's heart with the unction of His Holy Spirit, and makes him taste that *hidden manna* which is promised to those who resist temptation and fight manfully against their enemies.

That is a happy labour whereby safety is attained.—*S. Cypr.*

Covetousness.

WHAT crimes men commit while acquiring wealth, and what crimes with the wealth acquired! A rich man can do all he likes, and what evil likes he not? *They that will be rich fall into temptation and a snare, ... for the love of money is the root of all evil.* (1 Tim. vi. 9, 10.) He that is over-eager in the pursuit of wealth will soon be lukewarm in GOD's service. Other lusts grow weak with advancing years, this one gains strength; others are calmed when their object is attained, this is stimulated. It is like a raging fire which burns the more fiercely the more it is fed with fuel. A covetous man is also unjust, violent, hard, suspicious, knavish, without faith, without law, without affection, without scruples; he allows not the claims of relations, of friends, or of GOD. Self-interest is his only God, to which he sacrifices honour, conscience, salvation, everything.

Coveting money, a man loses faith; heaping up riches, he squanders grace.—*S. Amb.*

Lukewarmness.

LUKEWARMNESS is a state *neither cold nor hot*, a mixture of good and evil. A lukewarm person will not commit deadly sins, but he readily yields in trifles; he does not give way to violent ebullitions of temper, but is bitter of speech, peevish, and impatient; slanders not grievously, but yet backbites; hates impurity, but yet leads a self-indulgent useless life; covets not the goods of another, but parts not overreadily with his own. He practises good works, but without zeal or purity of intention; comes frequently to the LORD's Table, but without fervour or due preparation; makes long prayers, but inattentively and indevoutly.

So then he does what is right, but not in the right way. He acts under the influence of passing impulses, irregularly, and in a wrong spirit. He would be saved, if it could be done, without much trouble, and win heaven without *taking it by force.*

Remember, not the lukewarm, not the listless, but the violent take heaven by force.—*S. Aug.*

Christ's Love.

IN purchasing our salvation at such a price, our SAVIOUR would show us the value we must put on the glory of GOD, and how we must spare nothing to gain it. He would teach us the nature of sin and enable us to estimate its magnitude by showing us the magnitude of the remedy required; He would make us feel the exceeding greatness of His love by exhibiting the greatness of His sufferings, so that, as the ease with which He created us has furnished a pretext for our ingratitude, all He has undergone in order to ransom us may lead us perforce to love Him. *Christ suffered for us, leaving an example that we should follow His steps.* (1 S. Pet. ii. 21.) By His sufferings He has furnished us with a potent motive for patient endurance, and has earned for us assisting grace. The eternal FATHER says to each Christian, what He said to Moses, *Follow the pattern which was shown thee on the mount.* What we must above all imitate in CHRIST's Passion is the spirit in which He sacrificed all to GOD's glory. Mankind, blind, stupid, and intoxicated with vainglory, could not realize the nature of GOD, what He deserved, and what His glory demanded of them. It needed that One, at once GOD and Man, should teach them this by sacrificing Himself in life-long self-sacrifice to GOD's glory; by sacrificing earthly welfare, pleasures, glory, life itself. Christian, there is thy *pattern*. A SAVIOUR has given it out of love to thee; all thy happiness and glory lie in self-sacrifice to GOD, because thou art made for Him; the loss of thine all, sacrificed to His glory, gains for thee an infinite reward, and in losing all thou regainest all because thou gainest GOD Himself.

Let Him be firmly seated in your heart Who was fastened on the Cross for you. —*S. Aug.*

Born again.

THE resurrection of CHRIST is the pattern of our new birth; it comprises two things, a change of state, and an abiding in that state. So S. Paul says, *Likewise reckon ye also yourselves to be dead indeed unto sin, but alive unto God through Jesus Christ our Lord. Let not sin therefore reign in your mortal body.* (Rom. vi. 11.) Holy Scripture records three kinds of resurrection.

I. That of Samuel, who appeared unto Saul in a vision; such is the resurrection of so many Christians whose repentance is only in appearance.

II. That of Lazarus, real but imperfect, since he subsequently died: so rise many only to die once more in sins.

III. That of Christ, Who rose to die no more. Is this last a pattern of our own?

Christ's hidden love shone through His pierced side.—*S. Bern.*

Heaven.

THE love of God would have us be so strengthened by the contemplation of the bliss of heaven, as to endure the pains and persecution of the world, not merely patiently, but with joy, yea, with a joy akin to rapture. *Rejoice,* He says, *and be exceeding glad.* It cost Jesus so much to procure heaven for us, and we would have it cost us nothing! His cross, heavy though it was, appeared light to Him in comparison with the end proposed. (Heb. xii.) Faith teaches us that the cross is alone the way by which we may reach that end, seeing that it is the way traced out by Christ Himself, and yet we fear and avoid it! Heaven must indeed be a great reward, for it is the grandest exhibition of God's magnificence and munificence. He is rich and bountiful in all His other gifts, but here alone shall He appear magnificent. In hell alone shall He punish, in heaven alone shall He recompense, as befits the majesty of GOD. The evils of this life are but drops compared with the coming deluge of GOD's wrath; and present joys but drops of the torrent of delights in which the blessed shall hereafter bathe. If we taste so many sweets here in the place of banishment, what shall be the bliss in our fatherland!

When thou waxest faint, look to the reward.—*S. Aug.*

Bad Example.

A MERE spark has before now reduced whole cities to ashes. A smile, an immodest look, an ambiguous word, an undue exposure of the person, a bad example, sometimes lights a fire in some innocent heart which can never again be extinguished. Fathers and mothers, who give a bad example to your children, what an account shall ye render unto GOD! Ye have given natural life to your children only to slay the life of their souls! Alas! too, what an account shall they who have used their influence amiss have to give! Theirs are, as it were, original sins, which go on multiplying with an unhappy fruitfulness. Seldom is it possible to arrest or repair such evils; and yet, because they might have been foreseen and avoided, their authors shall not be justified before GOD.

Sins may be repented of, but the scandal remains.—*S. Bern.*

Occasions of Sin.

OCCASIONS of sin, sought or unsought, are to be feared. The greatest saints have ever dreaded them, whether caused by chance, or necessity, or the malice of the demon; nor did they think it unworthy of their Christian courage to grow pale at the sight of a danger which imperilled their salvation. David fell, because he allowed his eyes to fasten on a dangerous object which presented itself to them, unsought, unawares, and at a distance. What reason then have the young to fear, with passions strong, and virtues frail, with heart impressionable if not corrupt, with lively sensibilities and warm blood, if of their own accord they go in quest of dangerous objects! A man seeks an occasion of sin only because he finds some pleasure in it; he finds pleasure because the sin attracts him; the more it attracts, the more powerfully must it influence his passions and heart, and the feebler must his resistance prove. Is he not certain then to be overcome in a conflict in which he himself courts defeat? If he had not sufficient strength to prevent his placing himself in the way of sin, how shall he resist the attraction of the sin itself? If he was unable to stand firm, though unsolicited, on the brink of the precipice, how shall he arrest his fall when dragged downwards by the violence of his passions, and fascinated by their object?

Fly we then the occasion of sin, if we would avoid the sin. Furnish we them not with weapons against ourselves. The greatest saints have not disdained to seek safety in flight.

Joseph's weapon of defence was flight.—
S. Amb.

Frequent Communions.

OUR infirmities are no obstacles to our partaking of the Communion, provided they are displeasing to us. CHRIST invites to His divine banquet the infirm, the blind, and the lame, to show that *they* are not shut out, who enjoy not perfect health. By giving us His Body and Blood under the visible symbols of bread and wine, our common daily bread, He teaches us that our souls can no more exist without this spiritual food, than our bodies can without material food. How self-contradictory is man! GOD forbids him, on pain of death, *to eat of the tree of the knowledge of good and evil,* and he *eats.* GOD commands him, on pain of death, to eat of the Bread of Life, and he *eats not!* In this Sacrament we receive not merely grace but the Source and Author of grace—even the LORD Himself, who fills us with abundant outpourings of spiritual gifts, applies to *each* the price of His Blood, the virtue of His merits, and filling us with His Spirit unites us to Himself.

There is no presumption in communicating often, but there is in coming but once unprepared.—*S. Chrysost.*

Prayer.

HOW comes it that, although CHRIST has attributed such sovereign efficacy to prayer made in His Name, it is for the most part so ineffectual? Because we pray in a state of sin. A sinner who longs not for a change of heart, cannot use the prayer CHRIST taught without self-contradiction and self-condemnation. How pray, *Hallowed be Thy Name*, while he wilfully unhallows it? How, *Thy kingdom come*, while willingly serving sin? How, *Thy will be done*, while breaking His commandments? How ask for the *daily bread*—the Bread of Life in the Eucharist—only to use It unworthily? How beseech GOD to *forgive*, only to offend again? How seek deliverance *from evil*, when he perseveres in the greatest evil—sin? What a mass of contradictions! What a subject for condemnation!

But, secondly, prayer is not effectual because we ask for something wrong. Is it not a fresh sin to wish GOD to aid and abet what is wrong? Or again, we ask, perhaps, for health or worldly goods, which He foresees would be great obstacles in the way of our salvation, owing to their immoderate love or misuse. GOD hears in rejecting your prayers. What you think a blessing would prove a curse.

Thirdly, prayer is ineffectual *because we ask amiss*. We pray indevoutly and inattentively, and how can we expect GOD to hear us when we do not hear ourselves? We pray disrespectfully and turn our very prayer into sin. We pray without that lively faith which CHRIST has made a condition of acceptance. Lastly, we *faint* and wax weary, and perseverance is required to make prayer avail.

A petition is not offered in the name of your SAVIOUR, which is hurtful to your salvation.

Following Christ.

THOU bearest the name of Christian, but fulfillest thou the obligations? Thinkest thou that a little water sprinkled in Baptism made thee a *perfect* Christian? *That* indeed was necessary, but it is not enough. A Christian takes CHRIST for his example; the Gospel and life of CHRIST for his rule of conduct; he tries to become a lively copy of the Divine Original, so that he seems to reflect CHRIST in every feature, and to live the life of CHRIST. Art thou then a Christian? JESUS was humble, thou art vain and proud; He shrank from honours, thou seekest them eagerly; He was gentle and meek, and thou canst bear nothing; He forgave the heaviest wrongs, thou not the lightest; He loved His very murderers, thou not even thy brethren; He embraced a life of poverty, thou covetest the world's goods; His was a painful, self-denying life, thine is easy and self-indulgent; He denied Himself the most innocent pleasures, thou allowest the most dangerous and, perchance, licentious; He was *obedient even unto the death of the Cross*, thou wilt not obey in the easiest matters; He sought His own pleasure in nothing, thou in everything. Alas! the death of CHRIST will avail thee nothing if His life hath not been thy rule. His merits shall profit nothing if thou hast not profited by His example.

I am no Christian unless I follow CHRIST.—*S. Bern.*

Christ's hidden Life.

WHO can understand the conduct of CHRIST in His hidden life? He came to save the world, and He spent thirty years in a workshop, leading an obscure and apparently useless life. Why imprison such ardent zeal in a shop? Why hide such *a light under a bushel?* Why *bury* such talents? CHRIST seemed to be doing nothing, and yet what did He not while seeming to do nothing? When He was doing the will of His FATHER, was He doing nothing? When He was teaching us to understand that doing nothing, in obedience to GOD's commands, is worth more than the greatest actions done against His will, was He doing nothing? When, by His love of a hidden life, He was furnishing us with so powerful a remedy against pride and our love of ostentation, was He doing nothing? How His hidden life condemns us! We want to do, and take a part in everything, but it is to be feared that in doing everything we do nothing, because we do it not simply for God. It is vanity, self-love, and the desire of men's praise that moves us.

We sometimes serve God best when we stand and wait.—*S. Aug.*

Neighbourly Love.

THE first rule of charity is to love our neighbour as ourselves. We love ourselves tenderly. We feel the least evil which affects ourselves, and even magnify it till it appears great; we conceal from ourselves our faults, or at least represent them as light ones. We should do this in the case of our neighbour's also.

Secondly, we must love our neighbour

as we would in turn be loved. (S. Matth. vii.) Let us take our own self-love as a guide. Let each ask himself, Should I like to be treated in this way, to be addressed contemptuously, to be ordered about imperiously, to be maliciously slandered, abused, ridiculed, to have my lightest faults criticised and exaggerated, my most innocent acts receive a false colouring, purest intentions misinterpreted, conduct condemned on the faintest pretext, no allowance made for failings, no tenderness shown to faults? Should I not like to be treated in exactly the opposite way? Why, then, not observe the same rule myself in the case of others?

Thirdly, we must love our neighbour as CHRIST has loved us. (S. John xiii.) CHRIST has loved us when there was no merit on our part, when we were His enemies; He has loved us disinterestedly, poor and miserable; He hath loved even to the sacrifice of happiness, peace, glory, life itself. This is how we must love one another. (1 S. John iii. 16.)

He bewails his neighbour's troubles as though they were his own.

Conformity to God's Will.

THE *first* degree consists in enduring God's will with pain and repugnance, and yet patiently and unresistingly. There is no murmuring, but sometimes complaints, no opposition, but a wish that it harmonized with our own.

The *second* consists in submitting to God's will. We may feel repugnance, but we try to overcome it; we are saddened, but resigned. Complaints even are not heard, or if through weakness they escape our lips, are at once recalled and condemned; and stifling our rebellious thoughts we renew again the sacrifice of our own wills.

The *third* consists in *loving* God's will, even when it seems harshest. The greatest evils, when they come by God's will, become the greatest blessings, so that we should receive them not only with resignation, but with joy.

In adversity render thanks to God, and in prosperity confess thine unworthiness.— *Eucher.*

God's Presence.

GOD sees me! How the thought should curb passions, moderate desires, prevent sins, sustain courage, kindle zeal, rule conduct! He is ever present with me, ever watching me, ever thinking of me! With what respect and modesty should I behave in *His* presence, *before Whom the angels veil their faces!* Dare I, in *His* sight Who *cannot behold iniquity*, commit an action which I dare not commit before a fellow-man? He sees all the good I do, and will crown the least good work, even the faintest wish. He sees all my motives, and tests the purity of my intentions. He sees me when I am most powerfully tempted; cheers in the conflict; helps to stand firm, and displays the crown of victory. With what courage, then, should I fight! He sees me in affliction, all I suffer, and how I suffer; He sympathizes and considers my patience; is ready when I turn unto Him, to deliver, if it be for His glory and my salvation, or else to strengthen lest I should give way. *Why art thou cast down, then, O my soul?*

Angels, and the angels' GOD, witness thy conflict with the devil.—*Ephrem.*

The Measure of Grace.

THERE is a measure of *grace*, especially of those *strong influences*, which, once exhausted, can no longer be expected. *God*, saith the Apostle, *hath given us grace according to the measure of the gift of Christ.* GOD, infinitely wise, weighs and measures all He does; if there falls not a leaf except He will it, can we suppose that He leaves the distribution of His grace to chance? There is a measure of *sins.* However much the wrath of GOD is kindled against the inhabitants of Sodom, He says that He cannot yet punish them, because the measure of their sins is not yet filled. He promises to pardon the city of Damascus three transgressions, but He declares that the fourth shall fill up the measure of their iniquities and of His long-suffering. As there is a measure of iniquities, so is there of grace. The one is filled to the brim, when the other is spent. S. Paul calls the first a *treasure of wrath*; the other, *the riches of His goodness*. Does your waste of so much grace not make you fear lest your measure be exhausted, lest that one you are despising be the last vouchsafed? The measure is usually filled up by the abuse of some great, some special grace. The arm of God is stretched out to strike sinners, when it has been in vain stretched out to bless; an abundance of grace neglected is followed by abandonment. To whom was greater grace vouchsafed than Saul, when God chose him to be the first ruler of His people? But He was untrue to grace, and therefore he was abandoned by God both in life and death. How much grace was lavished upon Jerusalem during the sojourn there of Jesus Christ! It was the *time of her visitation* which, as He Himself declared, she *knew not*; and how terrible were the results! And thine own hardness of heart, after the voice of grace has urged thee so often to repent,—is it not a righteous judgment?

God Himself witnesseth that there is a limit and measure of sins.—*S. Aug.*

Salvation a hard Task.

SALVATION is a hard task; why disguise a truth which our SAVIOUR hath so plainly declared? He does not humour us in this matter. He speaks of it as a *narrow way*, along which *few* have the courage to pass, as a *strait gate*, by which it is so hard to enter in. Could He have made the truth more evident than He has? And in truth how many obstacles stand in the way, how many foes beset our path! Obstacles on the side of lust to be tamed, violent passions to be moderated, unruly senses to be mortified; inveterate habits must be rooted out, objects, as pleasant as they are fatal, must be shunned, dangerous occasions avoided, and strong ties broken. What firmness, what strength is required for all this! What courage is needed to combat the enemies which beset our path—the *flesh*, a traitor in the camp, to be feared the more in that we fear it less, the more dangerous the more we flatter it; the *world* corrupting us by its maxims, enticing by promises, carrying us away by its example; the *devil*, a foe powerful and cunning, watchful and cruel, making our perdition *his* great task, while we make not salvation *ours!*

Great efforts are required, and we do nothing! Constant watchfulness, and we slumber! We are called upon to fight, and we fly! Natural inclinations are to be *resisted even unto blood*, and we yield without a struggle! How does all this harmonize with a sincere wish to be saved? What! wish to be saved and yet do the very opposite of what is required! Were we placed on earth to work out our perdition instead of our salvation, should we not act as we do?

Your advancement will be proportionate to your zeal.—*Imit. Christi.*

Duty.

WHEN we serve GOD, we only do our duty,—less than we are bound to do, infinitely less than He deserves at our hands; and were it even possible for us to perform our whole duty we should still have to call ourselves *unprofitable servants*. The dignity of a king is more hurt by the slightest act of disrespect than it can be enhanced by the most respectful homage; and for this reason we may not do the least evil in order to promote GOD's glory—not even were the conversion of a whole universe our aim.

We may not excuse what GOD condemns.—*Tert.*

Hardness of Heart.

GOD and man contribute towards the hardening of the heart. Man begins the work, GOD finishes it. Man by committing sin, GOD by punishing it; man by resisting the light of grace, GOD by withdrawing it; at other times GOD chastises as a FATHER, but here He punishes as an enemy. There the result is often—penitents, here, alas! reprobates. A hardened heart is the beginning of a state of reprobation. It is blinded, not enlightened by the light. GOD's strokes, as they fall with an

Reverence in Church.

THE superstitious piety shown by the heathen in their temples shall condemn our irreverence in church; and yet they are only worshipping idols. Judging by *their* reverence, you would say that idols were gods; by *our* irreverence, that GOD was an idol. If GOD *smote more than fifty thousand of the men of Bethshemesh because they had looked into the Ark of the Lord*, (1 Sam. vi. 19,) shall He not punish heavily them that profane His sanctuaries? You come to church to appease GOD's wrath, and you kindle it afresh by your profanity. You come to declare your misery and needs, and you exhibit all the tokens of insolent pride! Inattention so sinful in your dealings with the Deity is perhaps the least part of your offence. Dare you address GOD in a *manner* and *posture* you dare not use to an earthly potentate?

Our chancels represent Calvary. With what sentiments of humility, reverence, and contrition should we enter them! Would you have joined your SAVIOUR's enemies to insult, and His executioners to torment

Him? And yet, do you not crucify Him afresh by your careless irreverence at the commemoration of His sacrifice in the Eucharist?

The most sacred rites are made occasions of sin.

Sufferings.

JESUS CHRIST, the Father of all mankind, made His will before His death. He left to the wicked the joys and pleasures of life; to the righteous, sufferings and afflictions! And yet the righteous have no need to complain. The joy of the wicked is often but in appearance, generally empty and ever brief. The sadness of the righteous, too, is often but in appearance; it touches the senses without reaching the heart. Without there may be trouble, but within is peace. Pleasures and friends may be taken away, but GOD remains. His presence outweighs every evil. The trouble is brief, for it ends with life, and shall be followed by changeless joys and eternal rest.

A Christian must suffer temporal evil, and await eternal bliss.—*S. Aug.*

The Love of God defined.

WE love God with all our *hearts* when we love nothing so well as God; and are ready to sacrifice everything rather than offend Him. This must be the aim of every Christian if he would be saved. Wouldst thou love and serve God and the world together? The love of riches, pleasures, and honours is incompatible with the love of God. Renounce then this love of the world, or renounce the love of God. God will not have a divided heart. He must have all or nothing. We must love God in everything, so that He may ever be the principal object of our love. Much more must we sacrifice to Him our unruly passions and sensual desires, subjecting our lower to our higher nature, and this again to God.

Again, we love God with all our *mind* when we submit mind and reason to His teaching, and make the knowledge of Him our principal study and greatest glory; and when we bear Him ever in our thoughts, Who never fails to think of us at every moment. Lastly, we love GOD with all our *strength* when we employ wealth, health, strength, and talents entirely, or at least primarily, in His service. Having received all that we have from Him, it is only just that we should show our gratitude to Him for all His benefits.

He is wanting in love to Thee, who loves anything *along* with Thee, which he loves not *for* Thee.—*S. Aug.*

Humility.

YOU shall meet with the patient, charitable, liberal, chaste, temperate, and meek, but where shall you find the really humble? And yet that man is not a real Christian who is not humble; while at the same time it is only a real Christian who can be humble. We can no more be saved without humility than we can without Baptism. CHRIST has said, *Except a man be born again of water and the Spirit, He cannot enter into the kingdom of God,* (S. John iii. 5,) and He has also said, *Except ye become as little children, ye cannot enter into the kingdom of God.* (S. Matth. xviii. 3.) Why then do we live as though we believed the one saying and not the other? The Gospel teaches us that there is no salvation without conformity to JESUS CHRIST; and that we cannot have this conformity without humility. Is not our pride a token of reprobation? Humility is a virtue which belongs to all sorts and conditions of men. It applies to great as well as small. The small are often humiliated without being made humble, while the great would be made humble without being humiliated. Self-humiliation is the surest means of securing our salvation; of gaining GOD great glory,—which rests on the self-annihilation of man; of rendering us like unto CHRIST Whose life was one long humiliation; of earning *His* love, given only to His followers; and of proving *ours*, by a sacrifice so costly. If we cannot bring ourselves to love humiliations like S. Bernard, let us have enough faith and reason to bear them without murmuring.

Humble thyself as thou wilt, thou canst not reach CHRIST's humility.—*S. Jerome.*

Mortification.

BAPTISM, saith S. Paul, represents to us the death and burial of JESUS CHRIST, Who engages us thenceforth to die to ourselves and to sin, and to live unto Him. Hence, this sacrament of life is a sacrament of death; it is at once our cradle and our tomb. (Rom. vi.) Living the life of grace, we are henceforth called to die to the motions of a sensual life and a corrupt nature. What else did all those Baptismal ceremonies mean? What those solemn renunciations pronounced on our behalf by those who held us at the font, and which we subsequently confirmed? Was it all an empty form, binding you to nothing? It was a solemn promise made to GOD, more binding than any other contract which can be made. And did you not promise to renounce the pomps and vanities of the world, and mortify all worldly affections? To crucify the flesh, repress all irregular desires, and renounce all sinful and dangerous pleasures? This is the essence of Christianity. A religion which falls short of this is a mere delusion.

Conquer self, and thou hast conquered the world.—*S. Aug.*

Besetting Sins.

TO war against his passions is the great work of a Christian. But he must not attack them all together; he must fight them in detail. The besetting sin must be first overcome; the victory over the rest is easy when this one is conquered. We must search our hearts to discover which is our besetting sin; which we combat least willingly; which sets our other passions soonest in motion; enters oftenest our thoughts and designs; creates the liveliest impressions and provokes the gravest disorders; which causes frequent and grave offences, and tends to greatest dangers and most disastrous consequences. This, doubt not, is our dominant sin. This one must be specially fought against, since our very salvation depends on the result. We must use every means, such as the consideration of GOD's presence, meditation, reading, the Holy Sacrament, mortification, avoid every occasion of sin, and practise self-examination.

Thou art thine own scourge.—*S. Aug.*

Backsliding.

EVERY fall enfeebles; but a relapse enfeebles still more, and increases the difficulty of raising oneself. When a man relapses frequently into the same sin, and abuses GOD's grace, he forfeits all claim to His aid. He has added ingratitude to sin. As Tertullian says, he thinks he may sin with impunity, because GOD is good, making His patience an occasion of sinning. He violates all his promises of amendment, under the pressure of the least temptation, to please, perchance, some fallen creature, and satisfy a shameful lust! Extraordinary grace is needed to restore such a man; but can he expect it without the most frightful presumption?

The very goodness of GOD increases thy sins; the abundance of His mercy emboldens thee in evil.—*Tert.*

Temptation.

ART thou tempted? Be not discouraged. GOD would try thy virtue first, then crown it. The Saint of saints was tempted. His example must be thy consolation and strength. Art thou tempted? *Fly*, if thou canst; there is no disgrace in flight; it is not cowardice, but prudence and courage. Thanks be to GOD for having given the victory—not to courage and resistance—but to precaution and flight. If thou canst not fly, *pray*. This is CHRIST's own command. The Apostles suffered the consequences of neglecting this command when, instead of watching and praying, they slumbered in the garden of Olives. Through neglect of prayer they cowardly forsook their Master. All our strength under temptation comes from GOD's grace, which prayer alone can obtain. If in spite of prayer the temptation continues, we must *fight*. GOD is watching us; He holds the crown before our eyes; He fights *in* us, and *for* us; what is there then to fear? The victory is certain if we do our duty. In this conflict we are never vanquished except by our own choice; while we fight defeat is impossible; as long as we are not defeated the victory is ours; and its reward is an immortal crown.

Then is temptation most formidable when thou perceivest not its advance.—*S. Jerome.*

Almsgiving.

THE rich man in the Gospel was not an extortioner or unjust, but he was a hard man. This was his crime. We owe tribute to GOD in return for all our blessings. He needs nothing Himself, He transfers His rights to the poor. Mercy is the only sacrifice which GOD now demands at our hands. All others were abolished by the new covenant. Alms are a debt which we owe to GOD; we rob Him when we fail to give them; we are His subjects, the poor His tax-gatherers, "their hands His treasury." (S. Chrysost.) The rich man is His steward, who robs his Master when he feeds not His household. GOD is the FATHER of all mankind. His providence feeds them. But He exercises His providence indirectly through the liberality of the rich. When therefore the poor man is defrauded of his dues you encourage him to question the gracious providence of GOD. *Your abundance* is *a supply for* his *want.* (2 Cor. viii.) The superfluities of the one, are the necessaries of the other. "That wasted bread," saith S. Basil, "that hoarded silver is not yours; if the beggar perishes for want of it, thou art his murderer, *non pavisti, occidisti.* His misery cries for vengeance upon thy hardness, and arms GOD'S very mercy against thee. If mercy itself condemn thee, where shall be thy refuge?" But, say some, the times are bad. Moderate then your desires, and you will have something to spare. Remember that as Christians you have renounced the pomps and vanities of the age, and you will find funds for the necessities of the poor.

Test thy faith; see whether thou canst lend unto the LORD, or whether thou canst trust thy slave but not thy master.—*S. Aug.*

The Magdalene.

WHAT fervour the Magdalene shows after her conversion! She sacrifices all to GOD—loves, pleasures, the world. GOD is now her all. Filled with thoughts of CHRIST, she forgets herself; and what has ministered to her sins, now ministers to her repentance. Her eyes, which have kindled impure fire in the hearts of men, she condemns to tears, with which she washes her SAVIOUR's feet, and wiping them with her hair, turns the instruments of past vanity into instruments of repentance. What fervour! Do *you* imitate her penitence, following the Apostle's advice, and *yielding your members as instruments of righteousness unto God?* (Rom. vi. 13.) A repentance such as yours, ought it not to be repented of?

Alas! the time when I loved Thee not, the days of grievous sin.—*S. Aug.*

Mortification of the Flesh.

THE first aim of mortification is the ordering of our pleasures.

I. First, we must cut off all sinful ones. For how can a Christian take pleasure in an act which robs GOD of His glory, and renders himself liable to eternal misery? Then we must forbid ourselves, as a rule, dangerous ones. For who would partake of a dish, however dainty, which had possibly been poisoned? Again, we must not allow our pleasures to become excessive or continuous. For they are remedies vouchsafed by GOD to our infirmities, and would cease to be such if they became habitual. Lastly, we must sometimes abstain even from the most innocent pleasures, because, (as S. Gregory says,) having fallen into sin through indulgence in forbidden things, we must raise ourselves by abstaining even from things lawful.

II. Secondly, mortification governs man's faculties and powers. It curbs undue activity and curiosity of spirit; regulates the heart's emotions,—its desires, affections, joys, fears, and aversions; represses the licence and wanderings of the imagination; stays our unruly and violent passions, and prevents their getting the mastery over the light of reason and the will, or if they break loose brings them back to allegiance, and punishes their excesses. Again, it restrains sallies of wit; watches stirrings of self-love, and silences subtle whisperings of self-complacency. Lastly, it keeps the flesh in due subjection to the spirit, checks intended, chastises actual revolts, treating it like a rebel slave which seeks to gain the mastery.

III. Thirdly, mortification causes us to submit to the cares and troubles of our station in life, its duties and responsibilities; to bear willingly crosses whether caused by the injustice of our enemies, such as calumnies, and persecutions, or by the justice of GOD using His creatures to punish and try us, or by tedious and painful diseases. It teaches us to bear all these in a penitential spirit, persuaded that our sufferings are less than we deserve; enduring, not with patience only, but with gratitude; rejoicing in that the empire of the flesh is losing its hold over us, the body of sin being destroyed, the old man being crucified, and we ourselves nailed with JESUS CHRIST upon the

Cross. This is what mortification comprises. Hast thou ever practised it?

Shall the flesh obey the spirit? Let thy spirit obey GOD; let Him rule thee, and thou shalt rule thyself.—*S. Aug.*

Trust in God.

THE LORD has promised that we shall lack nothing, and His promises fail not, but He attached to them the condition that we should *seek first the kingdom of God.* And that we are not doing. True, we seek at times GOD's kingdom, but not *first;* and that is the condition imposed, the neglect of which cancels the promise. "Think of Me," He said to S. Catherine, of Sienna, "and I will think of thee; be zealous in My cause, and I will care for thine interest; look to thy salvation, and I will look to thy fortunes." You are wicked and you want GOD to show extraordinary goodness towards you; you resist His will perpetually, and you want Him to regard yours at all times, and to take special care of a life which you employ but to offend Him! Was ever a claim more unfounded?

No such FATHER as GOD.—*Tert.*

Lukewarmness.

LUKEWARM persons do almost everything without reflection, or good intention, capriciously, under the influence of passion, through habit, out of regard to public opinion, or at the promptings of self-love. If they would only sound their hearts and candidly examine their actions, they would find scarcely anything done purely and simply for GOD's sake; and that vanity, the gratification of the senses, self-seeking, and self-satisfaction, nearly always hold the chief place. Alas! what shall be the astonishment of the lukewarm to find hereafter that, having laboured much, they have wrought nothing, because actions which have not GOD for their end, count for nothing.

Again, the lukewarm are negligent in acquiring virtues, overcoming failings, and practising good works. These are the three principal duties of a Christian, and yet they are often utterly disregarded.

Despise not little things, or thou shalt never do great ones.—*S. Jerome.*

Union with Jesus in the Eucharist.

THE tenderness of the love of JESUS is shown in His desire and endeavour to unite Himself to us in the Eucharist in a union the most perfect, the most admirable, and the most inconceivable. The Fathers compare this union to that of fire with red-hot iron. JESUS Himself compares it to that of food taken into the body, which is the most intimate of all unions, because by assimilation the former is taken up into the latter. *He that eateth My Flesh,* saith JESUS CHRIST, *and drinketh My Blood, dwelleth in Me, and I in Him.* (S. John vi. 56.) Is it possible to use stronger language? JESUS goes still further. He compares our union with Him in the Communion to His union with the FATHER in the Trinity. *As I live by the Father, so he that eateth Me, shall live by Me.* We, then, ought in our turn to show our love by our efforts to unite ourselves to Him by a lively faith, an ardent charity, and a perfect conformity of heart and spirit. This must be the result, yea, the infallible result, of a worthy reception. How comes it then that it is so often wanting? Because we place obstacles in the way. Two things cannot be united so long as anything intervenes between them. Our sins, our passions, our ties, come between Him and us.

Strip and bare my heart, O my SAVIOUR, of all things which hinder my desired union with Thee; strip me of them all, I shall be rich if only I possess Thee.

What better gift could even He bestow than Himself.—*S. Bern.*

Meekness.

CHRISTIAN meekness is not the result of a poor timid spirit, of a happy temperament, of good education, or of an innate sense of propriety. It is an excellent virtue, the result of a patience proof against all wrongs and injuries, a deep humility deeming itself worthy of all contempt, and a continual mortification of passions subjected to reason and grace. It is an outpouring of the unction of the Spirit, and sure token of the fulness of CHRIST's indwelling. Only a Christian can have this virtue, and he that hath it not, hath not the Spirit of CHRIST. A meek man feels anger when justly incurred. He allows anger to support, but never to get the better of reason; checks violent and harsh behaviour and banishes bitter and outrageous language; he may reproach, but not in offensive terms; all his wrath springs from charity and zeal, and not passion. The punishments imposed are ever lighter than the faults, so that the culprit, if he be not blind, feels that they are aimed at his *faults* and not *himself*. Do you observe this measure in anger? Think you, it is a good way to correct a fault, to commit a greater through the indulgence of immoderate anger?

Again, meekness smothers and banishes from the heart all resentment, not merely hatred and vindictiveness but even coldness and indifference towards the offender.

Far from giving way to offensive language, a perfectly meek man does not even complain; he feels the injury done to GOD, and the loss entailed on the evil-doer more than his own wrong. Not satisfied with pardoning the offence, he seeks pardon at GOD's hand for the offender; far from hating his enemies, he loves them sincerely, or rather he has no enemies except himself and sin.

Our King conquered the Devil through meekness.—*S. Aug.*

Penitence.

YOUR small dread of committing, or hatred of the sight of sin; your ease of mind after its commission; your indifference or insensibility under the loss of your GOD; the little eagerness you exhibit in repairing or recovering so vast a loss; your lack of courage in overcoming all obstacles to the attainment of this end,—all prove that you are very far from having a sovereign hatred of sin, and that you do not regard God as your Sovereign Good; since you do not regard evil, which is most contrary to Him, as your sovereign evil. How can you flatter yourself that you are truly penitent? What is your penitence but a delusion and a snare?

Hatred of sin alone creates true penitence.—*S. Aug.*

Repentance Delayed.

WHY put off your conversion to a future time? Are you sure of the future? God alone can insure you it. Has He guaranteed it? Has He not threatened the very contrary? How long will you keep saying with Augustine, a rebel against grace, "*Yet a little time, a little time*, and that little time ended not; *to-morrow, to-morrow*, and to-morrow came not?" Why not say with the same S. Augustine, now resolved to surrender himself to grace,— "How long shall I say, *to-morrow, to-morrow*? Why not *to-day*? Why not *this moment*?" (S. Aug., Conf. viii. 5.)

You need grace to repent; it is offered now and you reject it. Does not your contempt and misuse of it render you unworthy of it? The longer you put off your conversion, the more your sins will be multiplied, and God will be alienated. What can you expect from the anger of God? After living so long in sin you will need extraordinary grace for your conversion. Such grace is the effect of extraordinary goodness. Can you expect it from a God Whom you have so often despised and so shamefully outraged? On what then do you rest your hopes of ultimate conversion? Is yours not a blind presumption? Repentance requires a will strong and sincere enough to carry it out. The longer you delay, the weaker your will becomes; your sins multiply, your passions gain strength, bad habits get confirmed, reason yields, and mind is blinded. You cannot break with sin when it holds you by a thread, how will you be able when you are fastened to it with a rope?

Thou shalt have mercy on repentance, but shalt thou have time to repent?—*S. Aug.*

Holy Communion.

HOW careful should we be in preparing for the Holy Communion, in which our souls become in a marvellous manner the temple and shrine of the Divinity! Is there any religious duty more important than this? Behold! a GOD cometh unto us, the Saint of saints; with what purity and holiness should we receive Him! It was required of the priests, under the old Covenant, who partook of the shew bread, that they should be holy. What should be the holiness of those who so often feed on *the Bread of Life*. But how shall the Majesty of GOD join Itself to our vileness; His power to our weakness; sovereign happiness to misery; holiness to sinfulness? Shall not light sooner agree with darkness? Humility alone can effect this agreement. GOD takes pleasure in dwelling with the humble. The more I judge myself unworthy of receiving my GOD, the more He deems me worthy of this honour. And wherefore cometh He? To heal all my infirmities, deliver from all evils, cover me with favours, to give Himself unto me, and unite me unto Himself. Can I doubt His merciful designs when He works such miracles in order to come unto me? "*Open thy mouth wide*, saith the LORD, *and I will fill it.* I will carry My favours as far as thou canst carry thy hopes." If thy heart be empty, it is because thou hast closed it against GOD, through want of faith.

If the Eucharist be so excellent and so beneficial a mystery, surely nothing short of the impossible should ever keep us away from it! Are we not our own greatest enemies if we voluntarily deprive ourselves of the precious fruits there to be gathered by the application to ourselves of the merits of JESUS CHRIST? And with what feelings of lowly reverence should we approach! JESUS, both GOD and Man is there! He offers Himself unto His FATHER, and pleads His sacrifice on our behalf!

When thou seest the priest at the altar, regard him as the hand of the invisible GOD.—*S. Chrys.*

Humility.

TRUE humility should love contempt, for ought we not to love a real blessing? And is it not a blessing when viewed by the light of faith, since it enables us to sacrifice to JESUS CHRIST that which is dearest to us—our honour? We should seek it, because it renders us the objects of GOD's good pleasure and love, Who cannot but be pleased with so costly a sacrifice. It is a method of becoming like unto a God Who was despised and emptied of His glory. What a happiness! What an honour! S. Francis grieved at seeing himself honoured of men, counted it great gain when he lost their esteem, fearing lest it should inspire him with vain conceit. Nothing should humiliate us more than the fear of contempt and humiliation, when faith teaches us how much JESUS CHRIST esteemed it, and how eagerly He embraced it.

Love to be unknown and accounted nothing.—*Imit. Christi.*

The Elect.

"COME unto Me," shall CHRIST say unto His elect, "no longer to bear the cross after Me, but to reign with Me; no longer to renounce self and pleasure, but to enjoy all the pleasures prepared for you, and to be witnesses and partakers of My glory; come from the scene of your exile and enter into your fatherland,—from the abode of misery and tears, into the mansions of delights. Come and see if I deceived you when I said that, for the happiness which was being prepared for you, it was worth while to suffer every earthly trouble with patience and with joy. Come, My chosen ones, despised, persecuted, and accursed of the world, but honoured and blessed of GOD, My FATHER and yours; Whose benediction shall fully compensate you for all the maledictions of the world, since it gains for you a birthright, and an eternal inheritance with Me, Who, having willed to be your Brother, will now to share with you the price of My meritorious Blood. Ye shall be blessed in all ways everywhere and for ever; and, with Me, ye shall bless the FATHER of mercies, and the Author of all your blessings, throughout eternity."

"SAVIOUR, wherefore receive we this so great reward? For a morsel of bread and a cup of cold water! The reward, indeed, is beyond our deserts, but not beyond the infinite goodness of GOD. Happy they, O LORD, who endure much on Thy behalf, since so little suffering hath so great recompense of reward! Hapless they, and deservedly so, who willingly forfeit such a blessing when it may be bought so cheaply."

They who learn and gladly follow the teaching of the Cross shall not fear the sentence of eternal condemnation.—*Imit. Christi.*

Impurity.

MAN was created in the image of GOD, with a pure, spiritual soul. Through impurity all the features of resemblance are effaced and the soul becomes earthly and sensual. What an outrage it would be to cast the likeness of a king into the mire before his very face! And yet the unchaste fling their souls into the mire and soil their flesh, wallowing in brutal pleasures! This sin is great in the case of the heathen, but in a Christian it is a kind of sacrilege. CHRIST, being incarnate, became our Head, and we His members. *Shall I then,* saith S. Paul, *take the members of Christ, and make them the members of an harlot?* (1 Cor. vi.) As the Eucharist unites us still more closely to our LORD it greatly enhances the enormity of this sin in communicants. We become in it, to use the language of S. Cyril and other Fathers, one body and one flesh, and yet we dare to soil this flesh by indulging in shameful acts of uncleanness! Moreover, *our bodies are temples of the Holy Spirit.* (ibid.) *If any man defile the temple of God, him shall God destroy.* (iii. 17.) Impurity in the heart of a Christian is *the abomination of desolation in the holy place.* (S. Matth. xxiv.)

Take to your heels when attacked by lust if you would be victorious.—*S. Aug.*

Crucified to the World.

TO know the world is to despise it—so blind in its judgments, so unjust in its esteem and rewards. It regards neither virtue nor merit, and unworthiness is often a title to its praise. A true Christian must be not merely weaned from, but dead to the world. *Ye are dead*, saith S. Paul, *and your life is hid with Christ in God.* (Col. iii.) Men may be weaned from, without being insensible to, the world's good things. Without seeking, perhaps, they find their happiness in them. A dead man is insensible to everything. Splendid obsequies, magnificent mausoleums, the loud trumpetings of universal praise, are nothing now to him. They touch him not. There, then, is the picture of one dead to the world; there is the likeness of S. Francis Borgia. Though he gained the most splendid successes; though his virtues, his heroic actions, the marvels he performed, drew upon him the applause, esteem, and veneration, of the greatest men, he felt them no more than if they had not concerned him. He was dead to the world and to self. Insensible to all besides, he was sensitive only where GOD's glory was concerned. Happy deadness which makes a soul live to GOD! Alas! is my lively concern for my happiness and worldly interests not a proof that I am far from this blessed state?

All behind is but smoke to those who have GOD before their eyes.—*S. Aug.*

Sloth.

IDLENESS is the parent of many other sins. Nearly all sins of omission are its offspring. It is allied with a distaste for virtue, and great negligence in learning and performing duties, because difficulties have to be encountered, and courage is wanting to surmount them.

A common fault, it is little known. Men gladly forget distasteful obligations; or, if they remember, find a thousand pretexts, such as delicate health, the difficulty, or impossibility of the task, for their omission. The unprofitable servant in the Gospel was wholly blameless, it should seem, the fault lay altogether with his master! How many bury their talents, and hide them from themselves, to be saved the trouble of turning them to account!

Moreover the slothful deceive themselves in another way. Because their passions are not violent, and they are themselves too sluggish to undertake the commission of crimes which would demand great efforts, they reckon this very inability a proof of their own goodness. Pride often has a share in the sin of sloth. A proud man will attempt nothing, dreading ill-success, and the humiliation consequent on failure. Again, an idle man often mistakes for humility and modesty his indifference to the call of ambition, when his disregard proceeds simply from his fear of the trouble which would be incurred. He mistakes for temperance the little eagerness he feels in the pursuit of pleasure, though, at bottom, this arises from the cost at which the pleasure has to be purchased, and from his preferring indolence and sloth to all other pleasures.

Be not slothful, be not listless; eternal life is thy reward.—*S. Aug.*

Meditation.

HOW little faith there is among Christians! There is not indeed a total absence of faith; the verities of religion and maxims of the Gospel are not positively doubted, but they are taken for granted, not received with lively faith, not fathomed, not penetrated. And what is more calculated to make ours a living energising faith than the practice of serious reflection in our devotions? Surely the paramount importance of divine truths must make a deep impression on our hearts, (when we thoroughly realize them,) force us to put our hands to the work, and apply ourselves to the reformation of our lives! So that it may be said that just as want of *faith* is the cause of most sins, so want of *meditation* on the great maxims of the Gospel is the cause of our want of faith. Most men live without rule because they live without meditation. It is impossible to succeed in an important transaction, which is not only arduous in itself, but thwarted by powerful enemies full of vigilance and stratagems, unless the means of overcoming their opposition and defeating their measures are carefully sought. The Devil, knowing how important meditation is to our salvation, never fails to suggest many empty pretexts to deter us from its practice.

Some plead the engrossing nature of their business which leaves them no time. But can there be a more important business than that of our salvation? Others plead mental distraction which renders it impossible to fix their thoughts on any subject. But does it prevent their reflecting in any matter of importance upon the means which may be successfully employed, and upon the obstacles which may stand in their way? And why can they not do as much when their salvation is at stake?

A reflecting mind is the principle of all good.—*S. Aug.*

Repentance.

REPENTANCE is necessary, you admit; the Gospel teaches you that there is no salvation for a sinner without repentance, and you know that you are a sinner. But you await the hour of death to repent. "Ah! remember," saith S. Chrysostom, "that it is a question of your salvation." You make an affair of such importance depend upon a chance, while you take so many precautions in the case of trifles. But granted that you will have *time* given you and that your death will not be sudden, will you be in a state in your last moments to think of repenting? Are you sure of having a *mind* sufficiently free to think of so difficult a work? Shall a man whose frame is oppressed by the violence of disease, over whose senses a deadly lethargy has crept, whose powers are paralyzed, whose mind is prostrated,—a man overpowered at the thought of leaving all he has loved best, distracted at the sight of a thousand frightful spectres, in horrible suspense about his eternal future,—shall such a man, who cannot apply himself to the most trifling matters, be capable of giving himself to so important a business as a searching self-examination, and confession of the sins of his life, together with a lively sorrow for the past, and steadfast resolution for the future?

But, granting that your *mind* will be sufficiently free, will your *heart* be at liberty and sufficiently weaned from sin for repentance? For *this*, you must forsake sin, and not wait till sin forsakes you. A true penitent sovereignly loves all that he has sovereignly hated, that is to say, GOD, his soul, and eternal things; he sovereignly hates all that he has sovereignly loved, sin, the world, and the flesh. The covetous man must become liberal, the sensual chaste, the proud humble, the passionate gentle. Can all this be done in a moment? Can evil habits be changed as quickly as a garment? Not without a miracle of grace; and who dares without frightful presumption, rest the hopes of his salvation upon a miracle? Scripture mentions the conversion of only one thief. It was a miracle wrought in the presence of a dying GOD!

The means of conversion must never be put aside, lest the opportunity of correction be lost for ever.—*S. Aug.*

Idleness.

IDLENESS is the mother of all evil. It is also the teacher, saith the Holy Spirit. A man who has nothing to do is ready to do anything. He that has much to do has only one temptation to fear; he that has nothing, is open to all. The demon can attack him at a thousand points. This applies especially to sins of impurity. Occupation is their best remedy. Scripture declares that *abundance of idleness* (Ezek. xvi. 49) was the source of the sins of Sodom. What is the cause of the disorders of so many young persons? Idleness. Occupy them, and they will keep upright. Besides, we have so many calls of duty. They who know their number and importance only complain of *want* of time. They who have *too much* either ignore their responsibilities, or neglect them. Who can complain of having nothing to do while there remain so many mourners to comfort, so much poverty and sickness to alleviate, so many in prison to visit? Jesus Christ, whose members are left destitute, and whose altars remain bare, calls upon thee for help,—and thou hast nothing to do!

Always be doing something, that the Devil may always find you busy.—*S. Jerome.*

Temptation.

THE HOLY SPIRIT warns us that we must prepare for temptation as soon as we resolve to give ourselves to GOD's service. Nothing sometimes is more to be feared than freedom from temptation. It is often a sign either that GOD abandons us, or that the demon looks upon us as his own. There is no combat because we have ceased to resist. The greatest saints have been tempted. Had they not, they would not have been such saints. JESUS CHRIST Himself, being our *Head*, chose to be tempted that He might share our weakness, and impart His strength; being our *Pattern*, He would teach us how we must combat temptation; being our *Redeemer*, He submitted to this humiliation that He might merit for us grace to resist. So long as the *flesh warreth against the spirit*, we shall have to fight. Alas! LORD, I carry my greatest foe in my own breast. I am lost unless Thou fight in me and for me.

Temptation is frequently a trial sent by GOD for our welfare. He tempts us in order to test, and to display, our virtue. He tempts us to make us feel our weakness, and distrust our own virtue, and to force us to have recourse to Him, when the experience of our inability to resist such potent enemies imposes the happy necessity of flying to Him Who alone makes all our Strength.

He tempts, to purify us, for the HOLY SPIRIT declares that like gold in the furnace temptation tries and purifies a just man more and more. By it virtues are acquired and exercised; by it the heavenly crown is won, and we are kept out of that careless security which results from too protracted a state of peace.

To combat temptation with success we must, after the Apostle's advice, *give no place* to it; persuade ourselves that it comes from the demon as soon as it is felt; never parley, but start back from it as though we had touched fire unawares. When the temptation is one of impurity, we must not allow the mind to dwell on it under the pretext of ascertaining whether we entertained the thought willingly. A saint once asked how he should escape this sin, surrounded as he was by snares on every side. The answer was "Fly—fly quickly—fly far." We must exercise the greatest vigilance, realize the all-seeing eye of GOD, dwell on the Passion of JESUS CHRIST, take refuge in His wounds, *pray without ceasing*—an indispensable duty in the *moment* of temptation—and, lastly, never lose heart when we fall, but rise again with confusion of face, but with confidence.

Strength is imparted from above not to make us presumptuous, but cautious.— *S. Cypr.*

The single Eye.

THE first fault that creeps into our best actions is a slight self-seeking. Our only object must be to please God, and seek Him in all. Let us often ask ourselves, "Am I seeking God *only* in this action?" We may answer in the affirmative when we practise alike things smooth and hard, sweet and bitter, and when we positively prefer the more humbling and mortifying as often as we believe that so we shall please God best.

A second fault is to act on the spur of the moment, through caprice, or from a simple love of activity. The best actions, so performed, become imperfect. A Christian must act under the motions of grace, otherwise he often does a thing at the wrong time, and with undue haste.

A third fault is the trouble which arises from bad success. This springs from self-love and pride. We sought success for the purpose of getting praise. Had we only sought God's glory and His will, we had been at peace, for our humiliation is His glory, and His will is accomplished by our failure. Besides, as humiliation humbles us, it is better for us than a success which might have made us proud.

Seek Jesus in all things, and thou shalt

at least find Him; seek thyself, and thou shalt find thyself to thy cost.—*Imit. Christi.*

The one Thing needful.

HAPPY soul which, stripped and weaned from everything, desires and seeks GOD alone, and abandons herself entirely to Him! It is such a soul that S. Paul describes as *having nothing, yet possessing all things;* it is *that good part* which the Magdalene chose, and which could *not be taken from* her. Such a soul exclaims to GOD in a holy transport, " I place all my wealth in being stripped and weaned from all the good things of earth, too rich in my poverty provided I possess my GOD. I place all my happiness and pleasure in being deprived of all the pleasures of the flesh and senses, and all the pastimes of the world, provided I taste my GOD. I place all my glory in the absolute renunciation of glory and honour, if only by humiliation and self-annihilation I procure GOD's glory."

Such a soul has no other will but that of

God, no desires but *for* God, no hope but *in* God, no stay but *on* God. She would belong wholly to God, and desires Him to be everything to her—her wealth, her rest, her pleasure, her joy, her glory, her life, her alone and sovereign happiness. With S. Francis she can exclaim, "My God and my all." What is everything else to her? "To whom God is everything," said S. Francis de Sales, "the world is nothing." She enters perfectly into the feeling of David, and cries out with him, "*Whom have I in Heaven but Thee? and there is none other upon earth whom I desire beside Thee. Thou art the God of my heart and my portion for evermore.* Thou makest my delight on earth as Thou wilt make it still more perfectly in heaven." Such are the feelings of a weaned soul. You do not understand them, because you do not love. "Give me," said S. Augustine, "a soul that loves God, she understands all I say because she feels it; but to a soul that loves not I speak in an unknown tongue."

But again, what happiness does such a soul find in yielding herself entirely up to God! "Thou, Lord," she exclaims, "art more closely united to my soul, than it is to my body, and I repose on the breast of Thy Providence like a babe on the breast of its mother. May I not rest there in peace, and ever sleep tranquilly? GOD is ever thinking of me, may I not fearlessly forget self to think of Him alone?"

Having Thee, what more do we want?
—*S. Aug.*

Our Only Mediator.

"THERE is one Mediator between GOD and men, the Man CHRIST JESUS," (1 Tim. ii. 5,) Who came to reconcile the world unto His FATHER. *This* must be the foundation of our confidence. It is not on our virtues, were they even heroic, it is not on our good works, were they even perfect, that we must rest our confidence, but on the sufferings of JESUS CHRIST, Who by virtue of His Blood hath reconciled us unto His FATHER, *and hath broken down the middle wall of partition.* (Ephes. ii. 14.) The sufferings of my SAVIOUR have made satisfaction for all my sins, what then need I fear? They have merited for me every grace, what then may I not hope? However incurable my sores may seem, I have a remedy more potent than the disease; however countless my debts, I need not say that I have nothing to pay, since I find in the Blood of my SAVIOUR shed for me, an inexhaustible fund. Though, after the greatest sins, I saw the awful effects of GOD's wrath ready to fall upon my head —provided only I could realize a sense of perfect trust in the satisfaction of my SAVIOUR, and plead His merits before the Eternal FATHER—I should cease to fear my sins and His vengeance. For what can hurt me if I be hidden within my SAVIOUR's breast, which was pierced for love of me? Moreover, since my SAVIOUR's merits are mine own, there is no light or knowledge, however exalted, no grace, however extraordinary, which I cannot claim, and feel sure of obtaining, if I ask them with perfect confidence in the merits of JESUS CHRIST, because I ask them through Him and with Him—or rather, He asks them, O my GOD, in me and for me—and He justly claims what He has merited for me through His mercy. I dare even say, LORD, that

Thou canst refuse me nothing that I ask through the merits of this Almighty Mediator if I ask with perfect confidence in Him. And how shall I not when I remember what He hath paid for me?

The Mediator between GOD and man is a divine Humanity and a human Divinity. —*S. Aug.*

Recollectedness.

NOTHING is more necessary to advancement in holiness than recollectedness. The difficulties pleaded as an excuse for neglecting it show how needful it is. The more a man is scattered abroad, the more he has need to retire from time to time into himself. The best employments would otherwise tend to dissipation of mind. Things painful or pleasant, which present themselves in the way of our business, by arousing the passions, cause great distraction unless we be careful to return now and then into ourselves. The multitude of imperfect motives, too, which mingle with our actions when we are off our guard, di-

The Hidden Life.

vide the heart. The greatest saints have bewailed this tendency to distraction which they have recognised in themselves. S. Bernard, after having reproached a great pope with this fault, deplored his having himself fallen into it. But we do not lament it because our very dissipation prevents our feeling its effects or dreading its results.

The heart of man cannot exist without some attachment. To live is to love, and to love is to be attached. He must be attached either to GOD or to the creature. If he has not a spirit of recollectedness, which consists principally in the contemplation of GOD, he will not accustom himself to look for GOD in His creatures; he will not raise his thoughts from the creature and fasten his affections on GOD. Thus a man who seems zealous in all good works, and to be labouring with the single aim of detaching others from the world and the creature, shall find himself insensibly attached to them, owing to the neglect of recollectedness and vigilance.

Remember at times to give thyself back to thyself.—*S. Bern.*

Habitual Sin.

TO sin is a grave misfortune, but habitual sin is a still graver. It is easy to disentangle oneself from unaccustomed sin; it displeases even a corrupted heart in a thousand ways. But how rarely is an habitual sinner converted! It is a kind of miracle in the order of grace, of which the resurrection of Lazarus, after he had lain several days in the grave and had begun to stink, is a type.

"Habit," saith S. Bernard, "is a second nature; one changes in every other respect, but one does not part with one's nature and the habit of sin. Nearly all men act in accordance with their natural tendencies and habitual proclivities. Sin is readily committed, and iniquity swallowed like water."

S. Augustine calls a bad habit a slave under the empire of sin and the demon. Hard and cruel masters! "I groaned," saith he, "under the degrading bondage of my bad habit. My enemy had made a chain of my oft-repeated sins, linked together as it were, by which he held me shamefully enthralled. I struggled ever and anon to regain my liberty, but habit held me tight; and I feared like death to see the course of my sinful ways arrested, which were causing me to die daily. The evil, which had turned into habit, had more power over me than the good towards which I felt myself drawn; and the nearer the moment of my conversion drew, the deeper my dread grew." (Conf. B. viii. [v.] 10.) The habit of sin imposes a kind of necessity of sinning. Great is the misfortune of having the power of sinning; greater still, of using that fatal power; but greatest of all, of being unable to refrain from sin—and this is the result of a bad habit. "From an unlawful lust," saith S. Augustine, "we pass on to a sinful action; the action oft repeated strengthens the lust; the lust strengthened changes into a habit; and the habit becomes a fatal necessity,"—and yet a necessity which cannot be pleaded as an excuse, because it is not absolute, and because it is a result of our own wilful sin.

It must needs be an eternal torment to be eternally reminded of past sins.—*S. Bern.*

Excuses of Non-Communicants.

IT is strange that instead of seeking reasons for coming often to the Communion, seeing how great a benefit it is, we should seek reasons for absenting ourselves. One says, "I am unworthy." Are you then waiting till you are worthy? If so you will never come. What saint ever felt himself worthy? We are in a good frame of mind for communicating when we think ourselves unworthy and do all in our power to come in a worthy spirit. Humility supplements our lack of merit. If you renounce sin with sincere grief and a steadfast resolution never to commit it again, you are worthy. Otherwise we should be making *that* a *condition* of communicating which is its *fruit*. When the SAVIOUR administered the Communion to His disciples, were they already perfect? Another says, "I am so cold, so listless, so feeble." What! you will not come to the fire because you are cold? nor take nourishment because you are feeble? nor medicine because you are sick? What folly! If you are cold can you do better than approach this furnace of divine love? If feeble, strengthen yourself by eating the bread of the strong; if sick, take the efficacious and universal remedy for all the ills of the soul. Others complain of the small profit they derive. But whose fault is that? As a matter of fact, which make the greater progress in virtue—frequent or rare communicants? Perhaps GOD is hiding your progress from yourself to keep you humble.

It must however be observed that, while frequent are to be preferred to rare communions, it is a notion opposed to reason, to the sentiments of the Fathers, and the practice of the most experienced spiritual guides, to suppose that it is advisable or possible for *all* Christians to communicate daily, as some maintain.

If it is thy *daily* bread, why take it yearly?—*S. Amb.*

Sufferings improved.

IT is not a misfortune to suffer, since JESUS CHRIST says, *Blessed are they that mourn,* but it is a great misfortune to make a bad use of suffering. Sufferings are that Gospel treasure which few men find, or rather which all men find but which few turn to account, because they know not its value. (Imit. Christi.) "We find in the Cross," saith a holy man, "salvation, life, protection of GOD, abundance of spiritual consolations, strength of soul, joy of spirit, the epitome of all virtues, and the perfection of holiness." What wealth! And yet what Christian does not misuse it? The Cross is our life and salvation, and, through our own fault, we find in it death and ruin; it should be a source of consolation, and it becomes an occasion of discontent and murmuring; it should make our joy and our strength, and it plunges us into despair; it is the sure means of acquiring holiness, and we render it a subject of sin; it is the shortest path to heaven, and we make it a way to hell!

To turn sufferings to good account we must bear them patiently. Otherwise our crosses will prove worse than useless. If we bear our cross patiently it will bear us, or cease to be a cross; but if unwillingly, if we drag it along, it will overpower us. To suffer in spite of oneself is to have a foretaste of hell; to share the fate of the impenitent thief who descended by the cross into hell, while the penitent mounted thereby into heaven.

Where doth not the mercy of GOD appear, since even tribulation is a benefit? Prosperity is the gift of a consoling, adversity of an admonishing, Deity.—*S. Aug.*

www.ingramcontent.com/pod-product-compliance
Lightning Source LLC
Chambersburg PA
CBHW031346160426
43196CB00007B/752